FEEL, HEAL, RECEIVE

There is Healing in Feeling

A Journey Back to the Truth of Who You Are

By

Angela Hazelton

ISBN: 979-8-9988586-0-4

First Edition Printed in the United States of America

Cover design by Murad Aziz (@muradezizov)

Edited with love and support by Angel Evans

Formatted by Lucia De Humphery

Interior design by Angela Hazelton

Feel, Heal, Receive™ is a trademark of Angela Hazelton.

Dedication

To Gary Tyner Jr.,

A few days after you crossed over, I heard you clearly: "You have to speak, Miss Angela. The world needs to hear your voice."

This book is me speaking my truth, in love, and with purpose. Your words awakened something in me that had long been rising. The world is listening, and I am Grateful.

Acknowledgment

First, and foremost, I give honor, glory, and deep gratitude to the Divine Creator, the Source of all, the breath of life, and the Oneness in which all things are possible. Without this ever-present force of Unconditional Love, I would not be here, nor would this work exist in its truth and fullness.

To Gary Tyner Jr., Your words watered the seed. This book is the bloom. Thank you for speaking into me when I needed it most. Your voice still echoes through mine.

To everyone who has supported, challenged, and encouraged me along the way, thank you. Each of you played a part in this becoming. To those who reminded me of my voice, who held space for my healing, who believed even when I questioned, you are forever part of this journey.

To every reader holding this book: thank you for choosing to turn inward. May this offering be a mirror, a guide, and a companion as you feel, heal, and receive the truth of who you are.

From my heart to yours, Angela Hazelton

From My Heart to Yours by Angela Hazelton

To each reader,

I pray that you find exactly what you need during this interaction, when you need it. Whether it is gratitude, love, or forgiveness, know that this book is designed to meet you where you are, along your journey and experience, and accompany you the rest of the way, forever and always.

Our eyes are the gateway to the soul. Allow the words to connect within. Accept the awakening that it brings. Embrace the freedom that it gives.

Unconditional love is the answer to all questions. That is who we all are.

Receive, and Be the I AM, without apologies.

From my heart to yours, Angela

Preface

I did not set out to write a book to tell people what to do. I wrote this to show what it means to turn inward, feel honestly, heal intentionally, and receive fully. I wrote it because I live it. I AM it.

This book was born out of my willingness to face myself, to sit with emotions that once scared me, to forgive where I had shut down, and to love without needing anything in return. It is not another self-help manual. It is a lived example of emotional processing and the transformation it makes possible.

There were times in my life when I paused the movie. I pressed stop on my own progress because the idea of "feeling" was too painful. I now know that healing is not about avoiding feelings; it is about acknowledging the experience and allowing the full story to unfold. When we allow ourselves to process our emotions, the energy shifts, healing begins, and the truth emerges.

Feel, Heal, Receive is not about fixing yourself. It is about returning to who you are beneath the programming, fear and misalignment. This book may not be for everyone, and

I honor that. However, it is for those who are willing to turn inward. It is for those ready to meet themselves with unconditional love and compassion, embrace the lessons, receive the blessings, and honor the truth of the I AM within.

If these words have found you, I trust it is no accident. You are ready!

With gratitude and joy, Angela Hazelton

Table of Contents

Introduction

Feel, Heal, Receive is designed to guide you through a sacred process of reconnecting with your emotional truth, healing from the inside out, and opening yourself to the fullness of life.

This is not a book you simply read; it is a book you experience. Each section offers gentle guidance, reflective questions, and insights to help you shift from emotional awareness to soul-level alignment.

You will move through three core phases:

Feel: Learning to notice, name, and safely explore your emotions

Heal: Gaining clarity, releasing resistance, and rewriting internal narratives

Receive: Opening yourself to freedom, peace, authenticity, and divine truth

Along the way, you will also find moments of pause: Questions, reflections, and contemplations to help you process what is arising, in your own time. There is no rush. This is not a race. It is a return to you.

Feel free to move through the book linearly or intuitively. Trust where you are drawn. The words are gentle reminders, here to awaken the truth that already lives within you. The journey begins within, and I am honored to walk it beside you.

How to Read This Book

Welcome to *Feel, Heal, Receive.*

This book is an invitation to turn inward, feel honestly, heal intentionally, and receive fully. It is a companion for your journey back to yourself.

What to Expect

This book is divided into three transformative parts:

Part One: **Feel** – Acknowledging and Embracing Your Emotions

Here, you will learn the power of feeling and turning inward. You will explore what emotions are trying to tell you and create space for honest expression.

Part Two: **Heal** – There Is Healing in Feeling

This section guides you through emotional excavation, celebration, and the shift from conditional to unconditional love. Healing is not about fixing; it is about freeing.

Part Three: **Receive** – The Truth About Who You Are

In this final section, you will step into your power, rewrite your narrative, and embody your limitless nature. You will learn to live in flow, trust the unfolding, and create consciously.

How to Engage with This Work

Go at Your Own Pace

There is no rush. Some chapters may take a day to absorb, others a week to sit with. Honor your process and move through this book in a way that feels right for you.

Sit with the Questions

Throughout this book, you will find reflection questions and contemplations. These are not rhetorical. They are invitations to pause, breathe, and listen to what arises within you. Let yourself sit with them. Journal if you feel called. The answers are already inside you.

Allow the Stories to Resonate

This book contains personal stories: mine and the universal human experience. Let them wash over you. See yourself in them. Let them remind you that you are not alone.

Practice the Triple Bliss

Three core principles weave through every chapter:

- **Gratitude is the Way** – Let gratitude guide you home to presence and peace.
- **Love is the Answer** – Choose love over fear, compassion over judgment.
- **Forgiveness is Key** – Release what no longer serves you and reclaim your freedom.

These are not just concepts. They are the foundation of your healing.

Return When Needed

This is not a "one and done" book. As you grow and expand, you may discover new layers of meaning. Return to these pages whenever you need realignment, encouragement, or a reminder of who you truly are.

What You Will Need

- An open heart and a willingness to feel
- Patience and compassion for yourself
- A journal nearby (optional, but helpful for capturing insights)
- Trust in the process
- A commitment to showing up, even when it is uncomfortable

A Note from Angela

I wrote this book because I needed it. I walked through the fire of my own pain, suppressed emotions, and limiting beliefs. I know what it feels like to carry wounds you cannot name and to live in survival mode while pretending everything is fine.

But I also know what it feels like to remember who you are. To reclaim your power. To step into your limitless nature and live in alignment with your highest self.

This work is not easy, but it is worth it. You are worth it.

As you move through these pages, know that you are not alone. I am with you. The universe is with you. And most importantly, the truth of who you are has been with you all along.

You are a spiritual being having a human experience.

You came into this world knowing.

Everything is as it should be.

Let us begin.

With love and gratitude,

Angela.

Before We Begin: Setting Your Intention

So, I have a question... What brought you to this moment? What are you hoping to discover or heal through this journey?

Take a few deep breaths. Allow your thoughts and feelings to settle. Sit with these questions. Let them open something within you. There are no right or wrong answers. Just truth waiting to be acknowledged.

You might journal your response, speak it aloud to yourself, or simply hold it in your heart as you begin. Whatever feels right for you is exactly what you need.

The Journey Begins

There comes a moment when you can no longer outrun your emotions. You can try burying them under distractions, numbing them with busyness, or pushing them so deep that they seem forgotten. The truth is, unprocessed emotions never truly disappear; they wait. They linger beneath the surface, shaping our thoughts, influencing our behaviors, and manifesting in ways we do not always recognize. I know this firsthand.

I learned this in a uniquely challenging way. For five years after my mother's passing, I thought I was coping. I carried on with life, suppressing the grief and refusing to feel the weight of her absence fully. However, grief does not vanish just because we ignore it. It is waiting for an opportunity to show up and show out. On the fifth anniversary of her death, 9/6/2013, I found myself in a moment that I could not escape. My home was empty; all six of my children were gone, and for the first time in years, I was alone with my emotions. The silence was deafening. I felt the weight of something stirring inside me, something I had avoided for five years. All I could think of at the time was, Not Now! A still, soothing voice whispered, "It's time". I resisted, but the voice persisted. The voice was not loud, yet it filled the silence. It was not forceful, yet I could not ignore it. It felt like a quiet, divine invitation; a whisper from God, the Creator, the Universe, letting me know that I was safe and held. I did anything and everything imaginable to avoid the moment. I cleaned my apartment from top to bottom to keep myself occupied. My heart pounded, warning me that if I gave in, I might become consumed by grief. So, I cleaned. I scrubbed the counters, rearranged furniture that did not need rearranging, anything to keep the emotions at bay. However, as fear whispered, the voice persisted, calling me to trust the process. The more I ignored it, the stronger the pull became, as if my soul was crying out because it was no longer willing to carry this weight in silence. It was not just in my mind; I felt it in my body, a gentle release in my chest, a softening in my shoulders. The fear I expected never came. Instead, there was a knowing that the time was now. Finally, I surrendered.

I wept from the depths of my soul. My entire being trembled as I began to release the weight of emotions I had deeply suppressed. The only words I uttered were, "I miss her, I miss her so much." At that moment, something powerful happened. Instead of drowning in grief, I felt held by God, the Creator, the Universe, something greater than myself. I felt supported. As my tears slowed, I felt an undeniable shift within me; something had changed. I was not consumed by grief as I feared; instead, I felt comforted, guided, and completely safe. It was nothing like I had expected. There was no fear, guilt, or lingering pain, only surrender. The pain and suffering I had carried for so long finally passed, released through a door that had opened within me.

The space left behind was filled with unexpected peace, clarity, and unconditional love. I never felt the heaviness of my mother's absence again. Instead, her memory became a source of love, laughter, peace, and joy. At that moment, I finally understood that healing is not in avoidance, but in allowing yourself to fully feel and process the emotions you have attached to situations and circumstances. That day was the first of many that presented opportunities, resulting in amazing life-changing experiences.

Welcome to your Feel, Heal, Receive journey.

What a beautiful work you are.

I am so excited to share this path with you.

Reflecting on Your Own Journey

So, I have a question... What emotions or experiences have you been avoiding? What is your inner voice trying to tell you?

Sit with this question. Breathe into it. Let whatever needs to surface, surface. You do not need to have all the answers right now. Just notice what arises.

Consider also: What are you grateful for in your life right now, even amid any challenges you may be facing? Gratitude is the way home. Even in darkness, there is light to be found.

How can you show yourself the same compassion you would offer a dear friend who is struggling with difficult emotions? What would you say to them? Now say it to yourself. Love is the answer, always.

What judgments about your emotional experiences are you ready to release? How can you forgive yourself for any ways you have avoided or numbed your feelings? Forgiveness is key. It unlocks the door to freedom.

WELCOME TO YOUR JOURNEY

Welcome to your Feel, Heal, Receive journey.

What a beautiful work you are.

I am so excited to share this path with you.

Part One:

Feel – Acknowledging and Embracing Your Emotions

Chapter 1

The Power of Feeling

At an early age, many are taught that emotions are to be controlled, hidden, or even feared. "Be strong," we hear. "Move on." "Suck it up." "Let it go, don't dwell on the past." True strength is not found in emotional suppression, however. True strength is in having the courage to face what is within us, no matter what. When we deny our emotions, we do not just avoid pain; we prolong our suffering and delay healing. Suppressed emotions do not disappear; they settle within our minds and bodies, shaping our beliefs, behaviors, and even our sense of self. Healing begins the moment we allow ourselves to feel completely, honestly, and without shame.

Take a moment to consider the messages you received about emotions growing up. What were you taught about expressing feelings? About showing vulnerability? These early lessons, whether spoken or unspoken, have shaped how you relate to your emotions today.

The Cost of Suppressing Feelings

I used to believe that suppressing emotions was the key to strength. Over time and strained relationships, I have realized that strength without feeling is just an illusion. However, in reality, suppression only leads to suffering, and suffering, I have also learned, is optional. When we suppress emotions, we consciously push them aside, telling ourselves, "I will deal with this later." However, repressed emotions are different. They are buried so deeply in our subconscious that we may not realize they affect us. Whether suppressed or repressed, unprocessed emotions do not just disappear. They manifest in many different ways, such as anxiety, depression, unhealthy coping mechanisms, strained relationships, and even physical ailments. The longer we resist feeling, the more we prolong our pain and delay what is on the other side: Healing.

Feeling is Healing

Emotions are not our enemies; they are messengers. They reveal to us what needs attention and healing, as well as what needs releasing. The moment I allowed myself to grieve, I unlocked the door to emotional freedom. That is the power of feeling. It empowers us to process our emotions, release them, and move forward.

So, I have a question... What emotion have you been avoiding, and what might shift if you allow yourself to feel it without judgment or shame? Sit with this question. Let it move through you. Notice what arises. This is not about finding the "right" answer. It is about creating space for truth to emerge.

As you reflect on your emotional capacity, consider what you are grateful for about your ability to feel. Even the difficult emotions have served you, teaching you, protecting you, or revealing something you needed to see. How has feeling deeply served you, even when it was painful?

And as you begin to feel more deeply, how can you show yourself love and compassion? What would you say to encourage a dear friend on this same journey? Offer yourself those same words. You deserve the same tenderness you would give to someone you love.

Consider also what judgments about your emotions or emotional responses you might be ready to release. How can you forgive yourself for the times you have suppressed or avoided your feelings? Remember, you were doing the best you could with what you knew at the time.

Journaling: A Safe Space to Feel

I found journaling to be one of the most powerful tools for emotional processing. Writing allows you to express your rawest emotions without fear of judgment. You can put it all on the page without interruption. It creates a safe space where you can be honest with yourself, acknowledge your feelings, and begin to release them.

When I journal, I let my thoughts flow without censorship: anger, compassion, happiness, sadness, contrast, clarity, all of the feelings are free to flow. Afterwards, I always feel lighter. Journaling has helped me in so many ways. I recall a time when I was sad and confused about a challenging relationship, and just needed a safe space to sort out my feelings. So, of course, I grabbed one of my many journals. I opened it to a page, started reading before writing, and I was blown away! The words, feelings, thoughts, and emotions on that page were exactly what I was about to write. That journal entry date was almost five years to the day. I cried, and in that moment, I released so many emotions that I had attached to that relationship. For a brief moment, I judged myself for staying in a relationship that was not serving me five years after journaling about it. That judgment did not last long because my gratitude for and appreciation of those written words brought joy. That was a true awakening for me. I found strength that I did not know I had. Shortly thereafter, the relationship was over. I felt empowered by my own written words and my decision to move on. Journaling has always been a form of therapy for me, which is why I strongly encourage it to others.

If you are ready to begin your own journaling practice, try this simple emotional release exercise. Set aside ten uninterrupted minutes. Write freely about your feelings, allowing every thought and emotion to spill onto the page without holding back. Do not censor yourself. Do not worry about grammar, spelling, or making sense. Just write. When the time is up, take a deep breath and acknowledge your emotions without judgment. You might close your journaling session with an affirmation such as: I honor my emotions and know that my feelings are valid. I allow myself to feel and heal without judgment.

After completing this exercise, notice what you discovered about your emotions. How does it feel to give yourself permission to write without censorship? What surprised you? What relief did you find? These are the gifts that come from creating a safe space to feel.

Mapping Your Emotions

Beyond journaling, there are many creative ways to explore and honor your emotions. You might try body mapping, where you draw an outline of a body and color or shade where you feel different emotions physically. Or you could assign colors to your current emotions and create an abstract drawing or pattern. Some people find it powerful to write a short letter thanking their emotions for the messages they bring. Others create a simple timeline showing how their relationship with their emotions has changed over time. Choose whatever creative expression calls to you. The goal is not perfection but honest exploration.

The Power of Feeling

As you embrace the power of feeling, consider how this will change your relationship with yourself. What loving commitment can you make to honor your emotions going forward? Perhaps it is a daily five-minute emotion check-in, or journaling for ten minutes each day, or body scan meditations to notice where emotions live in your body. Maybe it is simply naming three emotions you feel each day. Choose one practice that feels accessible and commit to it for the next week. Notice how this practice helps you connect more deeply with your emotions.

Your Feel, Heal, Receive Journey Starts Here

Healing is not about fixing what is broken; it is about allowing yourself to process the feelings attached to the emotions so that you can be free. When you lean into your emotions, you return to your truth. Once you begin to process your emotions, you start to see that you are not your pain. You are not your trauma. Those were merely a part of your experience. You are something far more divine. You are a spiritual being having a human experience.

This is the beginning of your Feel, Heal, Receive journey.

As you close this chapter, reflect on one insight that resonated most deeply with you. How do you feel about beginning this journey of emotional awareness? What is one small way you can honor your emotions today? And most importantly, what does "feeling is healing" mean to you now?

Let us take these next steps together.

Chapter 2

Turning Inward

Many of us go through life believing that time alone heals all wounds. However, time is not the healer; emotional processing is. Unfelt emotions do not simply dissolve with time; they linger, shaping our thoughts, beliefs, and behavior in unrealized ways. True healing happens when we turn inward and consciously engage with our emotions, embracing the willingness to feel, acknowledge, breathe through, process, and release them, in and with love and intention. Turning inward means that you shift your focus from things external of you, to all things within you. Everything that exists in your current reality is a direct reflection of your internal thoughts, feelings, and beliefs. Let us turn the lamp on inside ourselves to examine inwardly and clear these emotional blocks. Of course, there is contrast within, but remember this: contrast is necessary for the greater appreciation of clarity. Understanding and identifying emotional blocks may not be as complicated as you think. However, it does require willingness and patience.

Take a moment to consider this: What have you been looking for externally that might actually need discovering within yourself? So often we seek validation, peace, or answers from the world around us, when the truth we need has been waiting inside all along.

What is an Emotional Block?

An emotional block is an unresolved energy that disrupts your ability to feel or express freely. These blocks can be rooted in unresolved childhood trauma or grief, fear of rejection, judgment, or failure, beliefs like "I'm not enough" or "It's not safe to be seen," repressed guilt, shame, or resentment, or the constant need to "hold it together."

Identifying emotional blocks is not about fixing yourself, it is about freeing yourself. While it may not happen overnight, it starts with willingness, honesty, and choosing awareness over avoidance.

Consider which of these patterns resonate with you. Do you often feel like you need to "hold it together" for others? Do you struggle to express anger, even when it is justified? Do you fear being rejected if people see the "real" you? Perhaps you have difficulty trusting others completely, or feel guilty when you prioritize your own needs. You might avoid situations where you might fail or be judged, or often feel like "I am not enough." Maybe you have trouble asking for help or support, or push people away when they get too close. As you recognize these patterns, ask yourself: What might these blocks be trying to protect you from? Every defense mechanism once served a purpose. Understanding that purpose is the first step toward freedom.

Identifying Emotional Blocks

If emotional processing is the key to healing, why do so many resist it? The answer is simple: we have been conditioned to do so. It is a learned behavior. From an early age, many of us were taught to "shake it off," "be strong," and "move on," yet we were not shown how to feel, express, or process our emotions. So, we suppress. We bottle them up. We deflect. We distract. We avoid. Not because we are broken, but because we were not aware that we were born with the tools we would need to handle life's challenges. Unfortunately, those who had the initial and the most impactful influence on us did not have their "knowing" nurtured. Therefore, they could not nurture ours.

Some believe that we might crumble if we allow sadness or anger to surface. Others associate vulnerability with weakness, avoiding emotions to maintain an illusion of control. Here is the truth: Avoidance does not erase emotions; it stores them. Everything we resist persists.

Emotional blocks are the invisible armor we wear to protect ourselves, but they also block healing, connection, and authenticity. These blocks are invitations, not flaws. Each emotion asks to be seen, felt, acknowledged, and at times, lovingly released.

Reflect on your emotional capacity and journey so far. What are you grateful for, even about the difficult emotions that have served as teachers or guides? How have your emotions, uncomfortable as they may have been, revealed truths you needed to see?

Consider also how you can show yourself compassion for the ways you have learned to protect yourself. What would you say to comfort the part of you that learned to hide emotions for survival? Speak to that younger version of yourself with tenderness.

And think about the messages about emotions you received growing up. How can you forgive those who taught you to suppress your feelings, knowing they were doing their best with what they were aware of at the time? This forgiveness does not excuse what happened; it releases you from carrying their limitations as your own.

Suppression vs. Repression: Understanding the Difference

While suppression and repression both involve pushing emotions away, they are distinct concepts. Suppression is a conscious choice. We actively decide to ignore or push down emotions to avoid discomfort. Repression, on the other hand, is unconscious. It happens when the mind automatically buries distressing emotions or memories beyond our awareness as a protective mechanism.

Understanding this distinction is crucial because suppressed emotions can be revisited and processed, while repressed emotions often remain hidden until triggered by an external event. If you have ever reacted strongly to a situation and did not know why, it is possible that an old, repressed emotion was triggered and resurfacing. The body and mind remember everything, even when we think we have forgotten.

Think about your emotional patterns. What emotions do you consciously choose to push down or ignore? What do you tell yourself when you are suppressing emotions? Perhaps thoughts like "I don't have time for this," or "It's not that big a deal." Notice these patterns without judgment.

Can you think of a time when you reacted strongly to something and did not understand why? What childhood experiences might still be affecting you unconsciously? Simply bringing awareness to these questions begins the process of healing.

How Unprocessed Emotions Control Us

When emotions are not processed, they do not disappear. They settle into the body and subconscious, becoming a paradigm. They influence our behavior in ways we do not always recognize. For example, unresolved childhood abandonment wounds might lead to an intense fear of rejection in adulthood, causing someone to push people away before they can be hurt. An old betrayal may result in deep-seated trust issues, making vulnerability feel impossible. By bringing suppressed and repressed emotions to the surface, we can break free from these patterns and reclaim our emotional autonomy.

The Body Keeps Score

Emotions are not just psychological experiences; they live in the body. Unprocessed emotions can manifest physically, contributing to tension, chronic pain, headaches, fatigue, and even illness. This is because the body stores emotional trauma in much the same way it stores physical injuries. Just as a physical wound requires care to heal, so does emotional pain.

Think about a time when you felt deep sadness, anger, or anxiety. Did you notice tightness in your chest? A lump in your throat? A strange feeling in the pit of your stomach? These physical sensations are the body's way of signaling that something needs attention. By listening to our bodies, we create space for healing. In that space, we recognize a profound truth; Forgiveness is necessary, not just for others, but as a gift of freedom we give ourselves. Forgiveness does not mean excusing hurt but rather releasing its hold on us, allowing true healing to take place within us. When we release resentment, we free ourselves. The weight that we carry is not solely about others. It is also about the space we reclaim within. Now is the perfect time to sit with your emotions and let the movie play. Do not press pause, stop, or eject. Emotions need to flow through us, not cut off mid-process.

To strengthen your emotional awareness, practice this simple mind-body check-in. Find a quiet space and take three deep breaths. Notice how you feel as you begin. Starting from the top of your head, slowly scan down through your body. What areas feel tense, tight, or uncomfortable? Your head and neck? Your shoulders? Your chest and heart? Your stomach and abdomen? Your arms and hands? Your hips and lower back? Your legs and feet?

For each area of tension, ask yourself: What emotion am I holding here? Simply notice what comes up without trying to change it. Then choose one area to focus on. Breathe deeply into that space for two minutes. What do you notice? How does your body feel now compared to when you started? What insights came up during this practice?

This simple exercise teaches you to listen to the wisdom your body holds. Your body is always communicating with you. Learning to hear its messages is a profound act of self-care.

Feeling Without Fear and Judgment

What if instead of fearing and judging our emotions, we welcomed them as guides? What if we saw sadness as an invitation to acknowledge loss, anger as a sign that a boundary was crossed, or fear as a call for deeper understanding?

Healing is about moving through the pain with awareness, grace, and compassion. It is not about avoiding pain, or hoping it fades away. Through it all, remember, Gratitude is the Way to all things positive. Gratitude is an anchor that allows us to honor what we feel while moving toward healing.

When we take a moment to acknowledge what we are grateful for, we shift our focus from what appears to be lacking to what is present. Gratitude opens the door to more blessings seen, felt, and received. Every emotion serves a purpose, guiding us toward deep understanding. Emotional processing is an act of self-love, a declaration that you are worthy of feeling, healing, and receiving the truth about who you are and all that life has to offer.

Feeling without judgment provides clarity, emotional resilience, and inner peace. We discover the ultimate truth in that space: Love is the Answer. This is not conditional love, characterized by attachment, expectations, and disappointment, but Unconditional Love, our natural state, defined by divine connection, allowance, acceptance, and freedom. If you realized in this moment, that you have been operating from the former (conditional love), simply acknowledge that current state as the contrast needed to appreciate clarity (unconditional love) more fully.

Consider how you might reframe your relationship with your emotions. Instead of fearing sadness, what if you welcomed it as a messenger bringing important information? Instead of judging your anger, what if you saw it as a boundary protector showing you where your limits have been crossed? Instead of avoiding anxiety, what if you understood it as your system's way of preparing you to face something important? Instead of suppressing joy, what if you embraced it as your natural state seeking expression?

From Avoidance to Awareness

This practice teaches us that emotions are not enemies but messengers waiting to be acknowledged. Healing is a journey, not a destination. With each moment of self-awareness, you choose love over fear, awareness over avoidance, and freedom over limitation. Keep going, your transformation is already unfolding. I encourage you to embrace your emotions as we continue this journey together. You are not alone in this. Your healing happens every moment you choose to feel, acknowledge, sit with, breathe through, process, and release what is no longer serving you. With every step, no matter how small, trust that you are moving closer to wholeness.

So, I have a question... When you get quiet and turn inward, what truth do you hear that you have been afraid to face? Sit in stillness with this question. Let the answer emerge naturally, without force. How can you hold this truth with love and compassion? What would change if you embraced this truth completely?

There are many creative ways to explore your inner landscape. You might draw a map of your inner emotional world, showing where different emotions live and what the terrain looks like. Or write letters to specific emotions, thanking them for their messages and guidance. You could create a visual representation of where emotions live in your body using colors, shapes, or symbols. Or make a timeline showing moments in your life when you chose awareness over avoidance. Choose whatever form of creative expression calls to you.

Consider committing to one practice this week to strengthen your ability to turn inward. Perhaps daily five-minute body scans, emotion check-ins three times per day, journaling about physical sensations and emotions, or practicing the emotion reframes when difficult emotions arise. Choose something that feels accessible and sustainable.

As you close this chapter, reflect on the most important insight you gained. How do you feel about the idea of your emotions being messengers rather than enemies? What is one small way you can practice turning inward today? What surprised you most about the body-mind connection?

This is the work. This is the journey. And you are already doing it beautifully.

Chapter 3

Identifying What Does Not Serve You

Many of us are unaware of the emotional weight that we carry. The buried pain, unprocessed grief, resentment, or fear that silently influences our thoughts, decisions, and relationships. These emotional blocks are barriers separating us from the life we truly desire. They tend to show up as hesitation in our dreams, distance in our relationships, or a persistent feeling of being stuck. To move forward, we must recognize and analyze them. Once that step is complete, we face a soul-searching task, asking ourselves, are these thoughts and blocks serving us? Afterward, for each one that is not, our work is to release them intentionally, with love and self-compassion. Then we can reconnect with the peace, joy, and freedom within us.

This beautiful work is individually ours, and we are worth each step taken. Trust and enjoy the process of discovering belief systems that no longer serve you, and releasing them.

Take a moment to breathe and honor your courage in choosing to examine what may no longer serve you. This takes bravery. This takes willingness. You are already doing the work simply by being here.

Recognizing Emotional Blocks

Emotional blocks can manifest in subtle yet powerful ways. Self-sabotage shows up as procrastination, perfectionism, or avoidance patterns that keep us stuck. Unhealthy relationship cycles emerge when we attract or remain in dynamics that mirror unresolved wounds. Resistance to joy appears when we feel unworthy or guilty when things go well. Emotional numbness creates a disconnection from feelings as a form of self-protection. And physical manifestations reveal themselves as tension, fatigue, digestive issues, or chronic pain that are linked to stored emotions.

A couple of pivotal steps in healing are allowing yourself to feel and becoming aware. Take a moment to reflect: Where do you feel stuck in life? What recurring challenges or emotional patterns keep showing up? These are often signs of deeper emotional blocks needing your attention and acknowledgment. Once you recognize these blocks, you can connect the dots to understand how they shape your emotions, behaviors, and physical well-being. Freedom is on the horizon.

Consider which patterns resonate most strongly with your current experience. Perhaps you procrastinate on things that matter most, or set impossibly high standards that paralyze you. Maybe you start projects but rarely finish them, or find excuses to avoid taking risks. You might downplay your achievements or success. In relationships, you may attract emotionally unavailable people, stay in relationships that drain your energy, or have difficulty setting healthy boundaries. Perhaps you feel responsible for others' emotions or struggle to trust people deeply. When it comes to joy, you might feel guilty when things go well, expect the other shoe to drop when you are happy, minimize good things that happen, feel unworthy of success or love, or sabotage good situations before they can hurt you. Emotional numbness might show up as feeling disconnected from your emotions, using busyness to avoid feeling, having trouble identifying what you actually feel, feeling like you are going through the motions of life, or using substances, work, or activities to numb things. Physically, you might carry tension in your shoulders, neck, or jaw, experience unexplained fatigue or exhaustion, have digestive issues that are not clearly medical, get frequent headaches, or have chronic pain without clear physical cause.

As you notice these patterns, ask yourself: What patterns showed up most strongly? Where do you feel most stuck in your life currently? What recurring challenges keep appearing in different areas of your life? Simply naming these patterns begins to loosen their grip.

So, I have a question... What belief, habit, or relationship have you outgrown, but keep holding onto out of comfort or fear? Sit with this honestly. What comes to mind? Consider how it served you in the past, how it is limiting you now, what you are afraid will happen if you release it, and what might be possible if you decide to release it. These reflections illuminate the path forward.

Choose one pattern that feels most present for you and explore it deeply. When did this pattern first show up in your life? What was happening when this pattern developed? How has this pattern protected you? What is this pattern costing you now? What would you do differently if this pattern did not exist? Understanding the roots and costs of our patterns empowers us to make new choices.

Imagine your emotional blocks as physical weight. If they were objects you had to carry, what would they be? Perhaps heavy backpacks, chains, boulders, or something else entirely. How heavy does this weight feel? Where do you feel this weight in your body? What would it feel like to set this weight down? What is one small piece of this weight you could release today? Visualization helps make the invisible visible, the intangible tangible.

Before we release what does not serve us, let us honor how these patterns served us. What are you grateful for about these emotional blocks? How did they help you survive or cope? Perhaps your hypervigilance kept you safe in an unsafe environment. Maybe your emotional numbness protected you from overwhelming pain. Your perfectionism might have earned you approval when nothing else did. Honor what these patterns gave you, even as you prepare to release them.

Consider how you can show love and compassion to the part of yourself that developed these protective patterns. What would you say to comfort the version of you that created these blocks for survival? Speak to yourself with the same tenderness you would offer a frightened child.

And ask yourself what you need to forgive yourself for regarding these patterns. How can you release judgment about the ways you have protected yourself? You did what you needed to do to survive. That deserves compassion, not criticism.

There are many creative ways to work with release. You might write a letter to the belief, habit, or relationship you are ready to release, thanking it for how it served you and formally releasing it. You could draw yourself carrying the weight of what doesn't serve you, then draw yourself free from that weight. Some people design a personal ritual for releasing patterns, such as writing them down and safely burning the paper, or burying it in the earth as a symbolic release. Others find it powerful to write a description of themselves one year from now, free from this pattern, exploring what that version of themselves feels like. Choose whatever approach resonates with your spirit.

As you prepare to release what no longer serves you, consider the specific thing you are ready to let go of. What three concrete steps can you take to begin releasing this? What support do you need during this release process? How will you remind yourself why this release is important? What commitment can you make to yourself?

You might affirm: I release what no longer serves my highest good, in and with love and gratitude. I am worthy of freedom from old patterns and limitations. I trust myself to release and create space for what I truly desire. I honor my past while choosing my present and future. I am strong enough to release what once protected me but now limits me. I choose growth over comfort and expansion over security. Or create your own affirmation that speaks to your heart.

Consider also what feels different about identifying these patterns with curiosity instead of judgment. What is one insight from this chapter that surprised you? How do you feel about the idea that your blocks were actually protective mechanisms? What is one small step toward release you can take today?

As you prepare to move into the next phase of your journey, remember: releasing what does not serve you is not about becoming a different person. It is about returning to who you truly are beneath the protective layers and misalignment.

What are you most excited about as you begin this release work? What truth about yourself is starting to emerge as you release what does not serve you? Trust what is arising. Your authentic self has been waiting.

Chapter 4

Releasing Emotional Blocks & Unblocking Your Emotional Flow

You have done the brave work of uncovering what has been holding you back. Now, it is time to release with intention, love, and compassion. The following practices are here to support your healing, not to pressure you. Each will help you move energy, create space, and reconnect with your emotional truth.

Go at your own pace. This journey is about progress, not perfection. You are already doing the work. Trust that every small step matters. Most of all, allow yourself to enjoy the process.

Before we dive into release work, take a moment to honor how far you have come. You have learned to feel, turned inward, and identified what does not serve you. That takes tremendous courage, and deserves celebrating.

Understanding Release vs. Deep Excavation

Release work is different from the deeper excavation we will explore later in this journey. Right now, we are focusing on creating immediate flow and movement with the emotions and blocks you have already identified. Think of this as clearing the surface debris so the deeper healing work can happen more effectively.

Release is about movement, not perfection. It is about creating space, not necessarily understanding every detail of why you held onto something. That deeper understanding comes later.

Tools for Release: Five Practices to Create Flow

The foundation of release begins with honest acknowledgment of what you are ready to release through inner work and self-inquiry.

Ask yourself: What emotion have I been avoiding? What belief is keeping me stuck? Journaling your responses creates a safe space for honesty and self-reflection. Let yourself write freely, without censoring. The answers that emerge often surprise us with their clarity.

Emotions are stored in the body, so mindful movement helps release them. To process your feelings, try yoga, stretching, dancing, or even a simple walk. Connect with nature. Movement does not have to be complicated. Sometimes it is as simple as shaking out your hands, rolling your shoulders, or taking a mindful walk around the block. Notice what your body wants to do. Trust its wisdom.

Deep breathing resets the nervous system and allows emotions to move through rather than remain trapped. Try the 4444 breathing technique, called box breathing. Inhale for four seconds, hold for four, exhale for four, and hold for four again. This rhythmic cycle helps regulate emotions and calm the nervous system. Repeating this a few times will feel like a small but impactful meditation session. Guided meditations focused on emotional release can be powerful in processing buried feelings.

Replace self-criticism with understanding and compassion through self-compassion and affirmations. It is safe to feel. There is healing in feeling. Affirm: I permit myself to release what no longer serves me. I am safe in my healing. Create your own affirmations that speak directly to what you are releasing. The words that resonate most deeply are often the ones we most need to hear.

Journaling for release takes many forms. Write a letter to your past self, expressing acknowledgement, gratitude, love, and forgiveness. List emotions that feel heavy, then symbolically release them. You might tear up the paper, release balloons, burn it safely, or simply say aloud, I release this, in and with love, because it does not serve me. The act of naming what you are releasing and consciously letting it go creates powerful energetic shifts.

The Role of Self-Forgiveness in Emotional Freedom

One of the most powerful emotional blocks is un-forgiveness toward ourselves, for mistakes, for not knowing or doing better, for past decisions made from ignorance, pain or fear. Carrying self-blame only reinforces suffering. True healing comes when we extend the same grace to ourselves that we offer a loved one or friend. Think of a time when you showed deep compassion to someone. Now, imagine offering that same compassionate grace to yourself. You deserve it just as much.

Forgiveness is not excusing what happened; it is choosing not to carry the burden any longer. It is an empowering act of self-liberation. It does not mean condoning the past. However, it does mean freeing yourself from its emotional hold.

Consider what you need to forgive yourself or someone else for that would create immediate relief. Sit with this question. Let the answer come without force. What would it feel like to finally release this burden?

Reflect also on what you are grateful for about your willingness to forgive and release. How has this choice already begun to lighten your load? What difference do you notice, even if subtle?

And ask yourself how you can show love to the parts of yourself that feel scared to let go. What would unconditional love say to these fearful parts? Speak those words of comfort to yourself.

So, I have a question... What would it look like if you gave yourself full permission to release what you have been carrying for far too long? Imagine it. Feel it. Let yourself envision a life unburdened by this weight. What becomes possible?

Try this breathing exercise for emotional release. Find a quiet space and light a candle or sit in soft lighting. Close your eyes and take deep breaths using the **4444** breathing technique: Inhale for 4 seconds, hold for 4 seconds, exhale for 4 seconds, hold for 4 seconds. As you breathe, visualize the emotion you are holding. Ask yourself, "Where do I feel this in my body? What does it need from me?" Place your hand over your heart and say: I acknowledge you. Thank you. I release you in and with love. I am safe now. Imagine the emotion dissolving, like smoke dissipating into the air. Close with gratitude, thanking yourself for being willing to do this beautiful work and showing up for your healing.

Notice where you felt the emotion in your body. What did it seem to need from you? How did it feel to acknowledge and release it? What shifted during this practice? These observations deepen your relationship with your emotional landscape.

When Release Feels Difficult

Sometimes emotions feel too overwhelming to release at that moment. That is okay. Do not feel pressured. You can always start smaller. Release just the surface layer of the emotion. Release your resistance to feeling it. Release the judgment about having the emotion. Release the pressure to release it perfectly. Meeting yourself where you are is always enough.

Creating Daily Flow

Releasing emotional blocks is a continuous process of self-reflection, self-awareness, patience, and unconditional love. The more we practice emotional release, the lighter and freer we become. Each time you choose to face your emotions rather than push them away, you take a step toward transformation.

Consider incorporating simple daily practices into your life. In the morning, ask yourself, "What do I need to release today to feel lighter?" At midday, take three deep 4444 box breaths when you notice tension. In the evening, journal about at least one thing you are ready to release before sleep. You might also practice body scans to notice where you are holding emotions, engage in movement practices like yoga, walking, dancing, or stretching, maintain a daily forgiveness practice, or speak release affirmations aloud. Choose practices that feel sustainable and nourishing.

Your healing is unfolding, one moment, one breath, one release at a time. Trust the process, and know that with each release, you are making space for more peace, clarity, and self-love.

Reflect on what has shifted in you since beginning this release work. What surprised you most about the release process? How does it feel to give yourself permission to release at your own pace? What are you most proud of yourself for in this chapter?

Consider what is the most powerful release tool you discovered. How does understanding that release is about movement, not perfection, change your approach? What emotion or belief are you most ready to release after completing this chapter? What does emotional flow feel like to you?

Now that we have explored the process of releasing emotional blocks, we will dive a little deeper. Let us explore emotional excavation, which is unearthing the hidden wounds that shape our thoughts and behaviors. The foundation you have built here will support the deeper work ahead.

Part Two:

Heal – There Is Healing in Feeling

Chapter 5

The Process of Emotional Excavation

Healing requires deep emotional excavation, the act of uncovering buried wounds, suppressed emotions, and hidden beliefs that shape thoughts and behaviors. This process can be uncomfortable at times because it challenges you to confront past and present pain. Nevertheless, it is necessary for transformation. Committing to the process is how you reap the benefits of true healing.

Acknowledge the Wound: Identifying past trauma is the first step to healing. You cannot change what you refuse to face. Whether it stems from childhood, relationships, or life events, acknowledging pain without judgment is a powerful act of self-love.

Allow Yourself to Feel: Suppressing emotions creates internal blocks, but allowing them to surface helps release their hold on you. Feeling creates space for healing.

Reframe Your Narrative: Trauma often creates limiting beliefs such as "I am not enough" or "I am unworthy of __________." Healing allows you to challenge and reframe these narratives, replacing them with empowering truths such as "I am more than enough" or "I Am Love."

Forgive and Release: Forgiveness is not about excusing harm but is the key to freeing yourself and others from its control. Asking for, giving, and receiving forgiveness takes willingness and is evidence of personal growth. Forgiveness releases the emotional weight that keeps you tied to the past. It is a gift of freedom and expression of unconditional love.

Take a moment to consider: Which of these four steps feels most challenging for you right now, and why? Simply naming what feels difficult begins to soften its edges.

Understanding the Difference Between Conditional vs. Unconditional Love

Love is often taught or displayed as something that has to be earned, measured, or dependent on external conditions. This idea can lead to unhealthy attachments, unrealistic expectations, disappointment, and pain. Understanding the difference between conditional and unconditional love is essential in healing.

Conditional Love: Often rooted in fear and control. Conditional love says, "I will love you if..." or "If you love me you will..." It is rooted in attachment, expectations, approval, disappointment, and performance. When we use love for punishment or as deprivation, it can create insecurities and emotional wounds. Unfortunately, this is the standard and example in most relationships, including parenting, friendships, and romantic connections. As a mother of six, I am all too familiar with this. I remember expressing disappointment toward my children, thinking it was the best way to guide them into doing 'right.' Looking back, I see how manipulative that was, even though unintentional. At the time, I did not realize how much pressure I was putting on them or how it would affect them in the long term. I just wanted them to do better in general. That hurts to type now, knowing what I know. I have apologized to my children and will continue to offer apologies as I support their willingness to feel, heal, and receive. The infamous line was, "I am so disappointed in you!" Disappointment is a clear indication that things are conditional.

Unconditional Love: True love has no conditions. It is accepting, allowing, freeing, and expansive. It does not demand, restrict, or seek validation; instead, it embraces you just as you are. Healing is the bridge that leads you to this profound truth. As you heal, you realize that true love cannot be earned, measured, or proven; it simply exists. As you heal, you begin to cultivate unconditional love for yourself, recognizing your worth without needing approval from others. You learn to release the expectations and disappointments that once dictated your sense of value. Your understanding that love is not something to be earned deepens, and you embrace the knowing that love just Is. When you embrace unconditional love by accepting, allowing, and freeing yourself from attachments and limiting beliefs, you align with your highest self. In this space, you embody and radiate a love so pure that it naturally attracts the same energy back to you. This is where authentic connections form, not from a place of lack or fear, but from the fullness of your being.

Do not get it misconstrued, unconditional love does not equate to unconditional access or tolerance. It does not mean accepting abuse, sacrificing your well-being, or remaining in relationships that dishonor your truth.

Unconditional love begins within. It is about offering yourself grace, while honoring your boundaries. It is about loving others without the need to control them and loving yourself enough to walk away when necessary. It is not meant to cage you, it is meant to free you.

When we shift from fear-based, conditional love to heart-centered, unconditional love, we no longer confuse love with control, validation, or sacrifice. We begin to heal at the root.

Unconditional love is not just a feeling; it is a frequency, a presence, a truth. It does not demand change or perfection;

it invites and welcomes acceptance, allowance, and alignment. Unconditional love says, "I accept you and honor myself." It creates space, not suffocation, freedom, not fear. Let unconditional love be the standard, not just the desire.

Become the place where others feel safe and seen. Also, the space where you are free to be authentically YOU.

That is the love you are here to give.

That is the love you are to receive.

The love that heals, Unconditional Love.

Consider your own love patterns. Do you often feel like you need to earn love or approval? Do you withdraw love or affection when disappointed? Do you have difficulty accepting love without feeling indebted? Perhaps you find yourself constantly trying to prove your worth, or use phrases like "I'm disappointed in you" with loved ones, or feel anxious when you don't meet others' expectations. Or perhaps you are learning to love yourself without conditions, can celebrate others without needing them to change, set boundaries while still holding love for people, are releasing the need to control outcomes, accept your imperfections with compassion, or recognize love as your natural state, not something to earn.

Reflect on these patterns. What do you notice about how you give and receive love? Think about the conditional love patterns you experienced growing up. How can you forgive those who taught you that love had to be earned? How would your life change if you truly embraced unconditional love for yourself? What would you do differently? And what are you grateful for in your journey toward understanding unconditional love? How has this awareness already begun to shift your relationships?

Shifting from Attachment to Connection & Freedom

As you heal, love no longer feels like something you must grip or chase. It becomes something you naturally embody and attract. You begin shifting from attachment, which is rooted in fear and control, to connection, grounded in trust and freedom.

During the healing process, you release the need to control outcomes or cling to people; instead, you embrace love as energy that flows freely. Love no longer defines your worth; it reflects it.

Breaking the Cycles of Self-Sabotage & Emotional Unavailability

Unhealed wounds often show up as emotional unavailability, perfectionism, or self-sabotage; quiet defenses that block you from the deep connection you desire. Healing interrupts these cycles and helps you return to the emotional safety within.

It empowers you to identify patterns. Recognize when fear-based habits, emotional withdrawal, or avoidance arise. Pay attention to how they appear in moments that invite intimacy, trust, or joy.

Challenge limiting beliefs by asking yourself: What am I really afraid of? Often, it is not love that scares you. It is the experience of being truly seen and possibly rejected.

Practice vulnerability. Emotional availability takes courage. It is not a weakness. It is strength wrapped in truth. This is where emotional honesty becomes personal liberation. You do not shrink here. You feel, rise, and show up boldly.

Think of a recent situation where you pushed someone away, withdrew emotionally, or sabotaged a good thing. What were you afraid would happen if you stayed open and vulnerable? Can you trace this fear back to an earlier experience? When did you first learn to protect yourself this way? Imagine what would have happened if you had responded with vulnerability instead of defense. How might things be different? What will you do differently the next time this pattern arises?

Extending Grace to Yourself: Self-Love & Compassion in Healing

Healing is not linear. It is layered, sacred, and deeply personal. There are no rules to follow, only rhythms to honor. There is no finish line, only continuous evolution.

As you heal, learn to extend grace to yourself. Release perfectionism. There is no "right way" to heal. Your best effort, in this moment, is more than enough. Speak kindly to yourself. Would you say that to a friend or family member you love? If not, do not say it to yourself. Honor your pace. Rushing the process only deepens the pain. Move at a pace that will honor your nervous system, your spirit, and your truth. Celebrate your growth. Every layer you release, every boundary you uphold, every emotion you acknowledge, that is the work. That is the healing. That is to be celebrated.

There are no setbacks, only lessons. Every lesson holds the doorway to a deeper blessing.

Consider how you will remind yourself of these truths. When you make mistakes, what will you tell yourself? When you feel like you are not healing fast enough, what will you remember? When you compare your journey to others, what will you say to yourself? How will you celebrate your growth this week?

Reclaim Your Power

It is often said that you are not your pain, your past, or the decisions you made while surviving. While that is true on a soul level, let us be honest, when we are still operating from unhealed wounds, fear, and survival patterns, those experiences define us. They shape how we show up, how we see ourselves, and how we interact with others.

If you are still making decisions from a place of fear and carrying the weight of betrayal, abandonment, or unworthiness, then yes, you are still living as the version of you that formed in those painful moments. Healing changes that.

Healing will invite you to see those parts of yourself, not with judgment but love and compassion. In that clarity, you reclaim your power. You realize that while your past shaped you, it does not have to define your present, nor dictate your future. You remember that you are not stuck in those old versions of yourself.

Healing reminds you that you always have the power to choose again: to choose differently, to choose from love instead of fear, truth instead of trauma, wholeness instead of woundedness. You may have experienced those things, but you do not have to dwell there. You can break the cycle, and reclaim your identity from pain. You can be the one who returns to the truth of who you are.

Healing is the act of reclaiming your power, your presence, and your truth. As you release the stories of unworthiness, scarcity, and fear, you make space for love, abundance, and authenticity.

So, I have a question... What emotional wound needs your attention, not to fix but to feel with honesty, compassion, and grace? Let this question settle into your heart. Notice what arises without rushing to answer.

Reflect on what you need to forgive yourself for as you excavate these buried emotions. How can releasing self-judgment free you? How can you approach this wound with love instead of fear? What would self-love look like as you do this work? And what are you grateful for about your capacity to heal? What strength have you discovered in yourself through this excavation process?

There are many ways to creatively explore your emotional excavation. You might draw concentric circles representing layers of yourself; from the surface to your deepest core; labeling each layer with emotions, beliefs, or experiences. Or create a split image showing yourself before beginning this healing work and how you envision yourself after. What changes? You could make a visual timeline of the emotional wounds you've carried and the healing you've done or plan to do for each one. Or write a letter to one of your emotional wounds, acknowledging it, thanking it for trying to protect you, and lovingly releasing it.

Consider committing to one practice this week. Perhaps daily journaling about one buried emotion, speaking to yourself with the same compassion you would show a dear friend, identifying one limiting belief and reframing it, or practicing vulnerability in one safe relationship. Choose what feels right for you and notice how this practice supports your emotional excavation.

As you close this chapter, reflect on what powerful insight about conditional versus unconditional love you gained. How does understanding emotional excavation change your approach to healing? What is one way you will practice unconditional love toward yourself this week? What old story or belief are you ready to release?

The work you are doing is sacred. Honor it. Honor yourself. You are uncovering the truth beneath the wounds, and that truth is beautiful.

Chapter 6

Celebration is a Form of Healing

losing the Celebration Gap & Receiving the Win You made it through some challenging parts. Now honor the "you" who did not give up.

We often think healing only looks like tears, solitude, or emotional labor, but healing has another face: celebration.

Acknowledging your growth, honoring your accomplishments, and pausing to say "Look how far I've come" is just as important to the healing process.

It is not arrogance. It is not self-indulgence.

It is spiritual alignment.

It is emotional integration.

It is receiving.

Take a moment to consider: When was the last time you truly celebrated yourself? Not for a birthday or external achievement, but for your internal growth?

The Celebration Gap

So many of us have been conditioned to push through pain but downplay progress.

We celebrate birthdays, weddings, and holidays, but what about getting out of bed after a depressive episode? Choosing peace instead of revenge? Having a tough conversation with kindness? Breaking a toxic pattern that has been in your family for generations?

These are wins. These are milestones. These are divine moments worth honoring. Yet, many do not celebrate them. Why? It is because we have internalized ideas like: "I should not need a reward for doing what I am supposed to do." "It is not that big of a deal." "I do not want to make it about me." "Other people are doing way more than I am."

This is what I call The Celebration Gap. The emotional and energetic distance between progress and praise. We move forward, but do not feel it because we never stop to honor it.

Consider which of these patterns resonate with you. Do you minimize your accomplishments, even when they are significant? Feel uncomfortable when people praise you? Quickly move on to the next goal without savoring wins? Celebrate others but rarely celebrate yourself? Believe celebrating yourself is selfish or boastful? Feel guilty taking time to acknowledge your progress? Compare your wins to others and decide yours aren't worthy? Think "It is not that big of a deal" about your achievements? Deflect compliments instead of receiving them?

Reflect on these patterns. What do you notice about how you relate to celebration? Where did you learn that your progress wasn't worthy of acknowledgment?

Why Celebration Matters in the Healing Process

Celebration reinforces healing in the brain and body. When we celebrate, we release dopamine, which creates a sense of joy and satisfaction. We also reinforce positive neural pathways and build emotional resilience. This increases the likelihood of repeating healthy behaviors and supports our knowing that life is not just meant to be survived, but deeply lived.

When you allow yourself to receive the win, you signal to your nervous system, "Healing is safe. Joy is allowed. I am worthy of good things."

This is the bridge from emotional excavation to personal empowerment.

What are you grateful for about your progress, even if you haven't fully celebrated it yet? How has your journey blessed you, even in ways you haven't acknowledged? Consider how you can show yourself love by honoring your wins. What would celebrating yourself with compassion look like? And what judgments about self-celebration do you need to release? Can you forgive yourself for minimizing your accomplishments in the past?

Receiving the Win

Let us own this truth: receiving is vulnerable.

To celebrate yourself requires presence, worthiness, and permission.

Many people do not struggle with healing; they struggle with receiving.

They can reflect, release, and repair. However, when it is time to rest in joy, love, and ease, the door is still closed.

"Healing is the journey. Receiving is the arrival".

So what does it look like to receive the win? Savoring a moment of peace. Documenting a small success. Sharing your joy without shrinking it. Affirming the work you have done. Rewarding yourself for how far you have come.

You do not need external validation.

You are the validator.

You get to say: "I did something challenging, and I honor that. I receive the joy that comes with that."

Think of three things you have accomplished or progressed in recently, no matter how small. For each one, notice what thoughts came up. Did you minimize them? Did you compare them to others? Then re-frame each win by writing why it actually matters and deserves celebration. Finally, choose one concrete way you will celebrate each win this week. Perhaps treating yourself to something special, sharing your win with someone who will celebrate with you, taking time to journal about what this accomplishment means, or simply pausing to feel proud.

Healing through Celebration

Celebration is more than confetti and cake; it is an act of reverence.

It says: "This version of me deserves to be seen."

So today, right now, take a deep breath and ask yourself: What am I proud of? What part of me has grown that I have not acknowledged? Where do I deserve to throw emotional confetti?

Healing is challenging enough. Do not skip the sweet part.

Reflect deeply on what you are genuinely proud of about your healing journey. What part of you has grown that you have not acknowledged? Where do you deserve to throw emotional confetti? How does it feel to write these things down and claim them? Allow yourself to truly feel the pride, the joy, the accomplishment.

A Loving Note

This is a gentle reminder that you are worth celebrating now! Not just when everything is perfect or finished.

You are worth it when you choose kindness over chaos.

You are worth it when you rest instead of self-abandon.

You are worth it when you rise, even if it is messy.

Celebrate yourself often.

It is not extra. It is essential.

Consider these affirmations and let them sink into your being: I am worthy of celebration, not just achievement. My small wins are sacred stepping stones. I give myself permission to receive joy. Celebrating myself is not selfish; it is self-honoring. I am the validator of my own progress.

Create your own affirmations that speak to your heart. What do you need to hear? What truth about celebration do you need to claim?

There are many creative ways to honor your journey. You might create a visual timeline of your wins over the past year or month, including both big and small victories. Or gather images, words, or colors that represent what you want to celebrate about yourself and create a collage. Some people find it powerful to write a letter from their present self to their past self, celebrating how far they have come. Others make a colorful list of twenty things they are proud of themselves for, no matter how small. Choose whatever form of expression resonates with you.

So, I have a question... What accomplishment, no matter how small, have you failed to celebrate, and how can you honor it today? Sit with this. Let a specific moment come to mind. How will you celebrate it? Do it today. Not tomorrow. Today.

Reflect on what you are grateful for about your ability to grow and heal. How has your journey blessed you? How has your growth blessed others? Consider how you will practice self-celebration as an act of love moving forward. What commitment can you make to yourself? And what old beliefs about worthiness or humility do you need to forgive yourself for carrying? How can you release the idea that celebrating yourself is wrong?

As you close this chapter, consider what is the most powerful insight you gained about celebration and receiving. How does understanding the Celebration Gap change your perspective on progress? What is one way you will close your celebration gap this week? And most importantly, what win are you celebrating right now in this moment?

Do not wait. Celebrate now. You have earned it.

Part Three:

Receive – The Truth About Who You Are

Chapter 7

Receiving the Truth, Owning Your Power, Living in Freedom

Healing is a gateway to transformation. It is the bridge that carries you from the wounds of your past into the limitless possibilities of your present and future. As you release pain, beliefs that no longer serve you, and conditioned limitations, you step into the next phase of your journey: receiving.

To receive is to embody the truth of who you are. It is about reconnecting with your knowing, owning your power, allowing abundance, and living with deep trust in yourself and the universe. Remember, we all came into this world knowing our purpose and power. However, over time, life's experiences acted as an eraser, wiping away our knowing and replacing it with the beliefs of others. Healing is not about discovering who you are; it is about remembering and reclaiming the truth that has always been within you. As we reconnect with our innermost, higher, and most authentic selves, we will rewrite our narratives.

Let us explore how healing creates space for receiving the life we long for. A life of freedom, fulfillment, and alignment with your highest self.

Take a moment to consider: What truth about yourself have you forgotten or buried that is ready to be remembered?

What Does It Mean to Truly Receive?

To truly receive is to open yourself on every level: mind, body, and spirit. Receiving is more than accepting external blessings like money, success, or love from others. It is a full-body surrender to life's abundance, both seen and unseen.

It is receiving rest without guilt, receiving clarity without needing proof, and trusting your intuition, even when it defies logic. It is receiving peace even amid chaos, and receiving love not because you earned it, but because you are it.

To receive presence, by being here, fully, deeply, without resistance.

When you are in receiving mode, you stop gripping. You soften. You open. In that openness, the universe meets you with everything you have been reaching for.

Receiving is not passive; it is an active choice to align with truth, open your heart, and walk in your divinity. It is a conscious decision to live in alignment, be available to all that nourishes your spirit, and release the belief that you must hustle, force, or prove your worthiness.

Consider your relationship with receiving. Do you feel guilty when you rest or do nothing productive? Struggle to accept compliments or gifts from others? Believe you must work hard to deserve good things? Find it easier to give than to receive? Feel uncomfortable when things come easily to you? Dismiss your intuition and look for external validation? Hold tension in your body, always "on guard"? Have difficulty trusting that good things are meant for you? Feel like you need to earn love, success, or abundance?

Reflect on these patterns. What do they reveal about your ability to receive? What blessings, big or small, are already present in your life that you may have overlooked or taken for granted? How can you practice receiving with more love and less resistance? What would it look like to soften and open? And what beliefs about worthiness or deserving do you need to forgive yourself for carrying? How can you release the idea that you must earn what is already yours?

How Healing Leads to a Deeper Connection with Your Authentic Self

Healing is about rediscovering your truest self beyond conditioning, fear, and external expectations. The more you heal the clearer you become on who you are, what you desire, and what you deserve.

When you are no longer carrying emotional baggage, you move with greater ease. You make decisions based on love, not fear. You create from a place of wholeness and abundance rather than lack. You love yourself without conditions, which allows you to radiate and receive love without expectations or limitations.

Try this remembering exercise. Think back to your childhood, before the weight of expectations and conditioning. What did you love? What made you feel alive? What did you know to be true about yourself? Then identify what was erased. What beliefs, traits, or dreams were dismissed, criticized, or discouraged? What parts of you did you learn to hide? Now reclaim your knowing. What truth about yourself are you ready to reclaim? What part of you is asking to be remembered and honored?

Based on your authentic self, not who you were conditioned to be, complete these statements: I am... I deserve... I am here to... Let these truths flow from your deepest knowing, not from what others told you or what you think you should say.

Signs You Are Reconnecting with Your Authentic Self

As you reconnect with your authentic self, you feel lighter, like a weight you did not even realize you were carrying has been lifted. Life flows more efficiently, and your intuition speaks with clarity. You trust it now, no longer searching for external validation. Setting boundaries feels natural rather than daunting. It becomes a natural extension of self-respect; you no longer shrink yourself to fit into spaces that do not honor or serve you. Instead of resisting life's twists and turns, you embrace your journey, knowing that every experience shapes you in the best way possible. As you align more deeply with your authentic self, life begins to unfold with grace and ease. You stop chasing and start attracting. You stop forcing and begin flowing. What is meant for you does not pass you by it finds you because you have finally found yourself.

Notice which of these signs you are already experiencing. Do you feel lighter and more at peace? Is your intuition clearer and stronger? Do you trust yourself more than you used to? Does setting boundaries feel easier and more natural? Are you less reactive to others' opinions? Do you feel more aligned with your purpose? Are you attracting people and opportunities that resonate with your truth? Can you be yourself without apologizing or explaining? Do you feel more joy and ease in daily life?

Celebrate these shifts. Which feel most significant to you? How do they change your day-to-day experience?

So, I have a question... Where in your life are you still rejecting what is already yours to receive? Sit with this honestly. Where are you blocking your own blessings? Where are you saying no to what wants to come to you?

Reflect on what you are most grateful for about the journey of remembering who you truly are. How has healing opened you to receive more? Consider how you can love yourself more deeply as you step into your power and freedom. What does unconditional self-love look like for you now? And ask yourself what you need to forgive yourself for in order to fully receive your truth and power. What old stories are you ready to release?

There are many creative ways to honor your authentic self. You might draw or describe yourself before healing and after reconnecting with your authentic self, noting what has changed. Or create a visual collage of images and words that represent who you truly are and what you are here to receive. Some people write a letter from their most authentic, healed self to their current self, offering guidance and encouragement. Others create a visual timeline showing moments when they forgot themselves and moments when they remembered their truth. Choose what speaks to your soul.

Consider these power declarations and let them anchor into your being: I am ready to receive all that is meant for me. I trust my intuition and honor my inner knowing. I am worthy of love, abundance, and freedom simply because I exist. I release the need to prove, perform, or hustle for my worthiness. I am remembering who I was before the world told me who to be.

Commit to one practice this week that supports your receiving. Perhaps daily morning meditation connecting with your authentic self, journaling about one truth you are reclaiming each day, practicing receiving without guilt, trusting your intuition on at least one decision daily, or setting one boundary that honors your authentic self. Choose what feels aligned and notice how it shifts your experience.

As you close this chapter, reflect on the most powerful truth about yourself that you are ready to receive and embody. How does understanding receiving as an active choice change your perspective? What is one way you will practice opening to receive this week? What part of your authentic self are you most excited to reclaim?

You are remembering. You are receiving. You are becoming who you have always been. This is the truth of your divine nature revealing itself.

Chapter 8

Rewriting Your Narrative

Your past does not define you, but the story you tell yourself about it does. If healing is the process of clearing out limiting beliefs, then receiving is the act of replacing them with empowering truths.

Healing asks: What wounds and experiences have shaped my beliefs about myself?

Receiving asks: Who am I beyond those wounds and because of those experiences?

Now is the time to rewrite your story with a narrative that reflects your strength, resilience, and infinite worth.

Now that you are ready to embrace your truth, let us explore how to reframe your internal dialogue.

Take a moment to consider: What story have you been telling yourself about who you are that is ready to be rewritten?

Creating a New, Empowering Belief System

Challenge old narratives. Every time you hear a limiting belief (e.g., "I am not enough"), replace it with a new truth ("I am worthy of everything I desire").

Use affirmations intentionally. Words shape reality. If you change what you say, you will change what you see. Speak life into yourself daily.

Visualize your highest self. See yourself free, thriving, successful, and at peace, then embody that energy now. Sit with that feeling, that knowing. Embrace and honor it as if it is already your reality.

Take aligned action. New beliefs must be reinforced with action. Choose thoughts, habits, and decisions that reflect your worth. When you own your new narrative, you step into the reality you were always meant to live.

Try this narrative rewrite exercise. First, identify your old narratives. What limiting beliefs have you been carrying about yourself? Write them without judgment. Then trace the origin. For each belief, ask: Where did this belief come from? Who or what taught me this? Next, challenge the belief. Is this belief actually true, or is it just a story you have been telling yourself? What evidence contradicts this belief? Then write your new truth. Replace each limiting belief with an empowering truth that reflects who you truly are. Finally, embody your new truth. How will you reinforce these new truths through your thoughts, words, and actions this week?

As you do this work, reflect on what you are grateful for about your ability to rewrite your narrative. How has your journey equipped you to create new beliefs? Consider how you can speak to yourself with more love as you create these new beliefs. What would unconditional self-love sound like? And ask yourself what old narratives you need to forgive yourself for believing. How can you release judgment about the stories you once told yourself?

The Art of Allowing: Receiving Abundance, Love, and Fulfillment

Many people unknowingly block their blessings by denying what they desire. Receiving is about allowing what you desire to flow to and through you with ease and accepting it with gratitude and appreciation. True receiving is about being in alignment, knowing that everything already exists and is revealing itself to you. The art of allowing means you do not chase, force, or cling. Instead, you align, trust, and attract.

The Key to Receiving:

Believe you are worthy. The universe cannot give you what you do not feel worthy of having. It will continue to provide more of what you give your energy and attention to.

Release control. Stop micromanaging how things "should" happen. Release the attachment to the expectations of timelines and outcomes.

Stay open. Blessings often come in unexpected ways. Be flexible in how you receive. Keep your mind open to everything and attached to nothing.

Practice gratitude.

Remember, Gratitude is the Way! The more you appreciate what you have, the more you will see things to appreciate. You will invite abundance, effortlessly.

When you step into the art of allowing, you open yourself to receive love, opportunities, and experiences that match your energy.

Consider the ways you may be blocking your blessings. Do you dismiss compliments or downplay your achievements? Feel guilty when good things happen to you? Sabotage opportunities that feel "too good to be true"? Struggle to ask for or accept help from others? Focus more on what is missing than what is present? Control how and when things should happen? Doubt that you deserve good things? Stay busy to avoid receiving rest or peace? Reject opportunities because of fear or unworthiness?

Reflect on these blocks. What pattern do you notice? How might these blocks be protecting you from something? And more importantly, what would open if you released them?

Complete these allowing statements from your heart: I am worthy of receiving... I release control over... I am open to receiving in unexpected ways, such as... I am grateful for what I already have, including... One way I will practice allowing this week is...

Living as a Limitless Being: A New Perspective on Life and Purpose

You are not to live small, hide in the background, and play it safe. You are not to live in fear, scarcity, or self-doubt. Your mere existence is of bold and confident design, on and for a purpose. Own that, and operate from the place of knowing.

To receive fully, you must embrace the truth: You are a Spiritual being, which makes you limitless; your potential is infinite. You are capable of creating, doing, being, having and becoming anything you desire.

Living as a limitless being means operating from love and abundance, not fear. It means knowing that you do not need permission to take up space. You are not bound to past circumstances or societal expectations. You create your reality through your beliefs, energy, knowing and actions.

When you fully step into your limitless nature, you move through life with freedom, confidence, and joy. You stop settling for less than you deserve. You receive the love, success, and peace that have always existed within you.

Speak these limitless declarations with power: I am a limitless being. My potential is infinite. I am capable of creating, doing, being, having, and becoming anything I desire. I do not need permission to take up space. I create my reality through my beliefs, energy, knowing, and actions.

Let these truths reverberate through your entire being. You are not speaking wishful thinking. You are claiming what has always been true.

There are many ways to creatively embody your new narrative. You might create a visual representation of your limitless life, including images, words, and symbols that represent who you are becoming. Or write a letter from your future limitless self to your present self, describing the life you are now living. Some people create two columns showing their old limiting narrative on one side and their new empowering narrative on the other. Others draw a map of their life as a limitless being, showing what their day looks like, their relationships, their work, their joy. Choose what resonates with your creative spirit.

So, I have a question... What is one limiting belief you are ready to rewrite, and what new truth are you choosing to live by instead? Name the old belief clearly. Then declare your new empowering truth with conviction. How will this new truth change the way you show up in your life? Envision it. Feel it. Embody it now.

Reflect on what you are grateful for about your power to rewrite your story. How does gratitude amplify your ability to receive? Consider how you will love yourself more fully as you step into your limitless nature. What does loving yourself without limits look like? And ask yourself what you need to forgive yourself for in order to fully embrace your limitless potential. What fears or doubts are you ready to release?

Commit to one practice this week that helps you embody your new narrative. Perhaps daily affirmations speaking your new truths aloud, visualization practice seeing your limitless self, challenging one limiting belief each day and replacing it, practicing the art of allowing by releasing control, or journaling about your limitless potential. Choose what feels aligned and watch how it shifts your reality.

As you close this chapter, reflect on the most powerful realization you had about rewriting your narrative. How does seeing yourself as a limitless being change your perspective on life? What is one action you will take this week that reflects your new empowering belief? What does living as a limitless being look like for you?

You are rewriting your story. Not with force, but with truth. Not with struggle, but with surrender to who you have always been. This is your narrative. Own it. Live it. Be it.

Chapter 9

Embody – The "I Am" in You

Sustaining Freedom, Abundance, and Alignment

Once you have reclaimed your power, rewritten your story, and embraced your limitlessness, the next step is daily embodiment.

To sustain freedom, abundance, and alignment, you must make them a way of life. Integration happens when you move beyond understanding and belief, into embodying these truths from a place of deep knowing. This unfolds through your thoughts, your choices, and the way you show up in the world.

Let us explore how to remain in a state of knowing, prevent self-sabotage, and nurture the life you have decided to accept, allow, and embrace.

Take a moment to consider: What is the difference between knowing something intellectually and embodying it in every cell of your being?

The Power of Integration: Making Transformation a Lifestyle

Transformation does not happen in a single moment. It unfolds through a daily commitment to living your truth. Feeling, Healing, and Receiving are not events; they are an ongoing process of deepening your connection to yourself and the universe.

Ways to Integrate Your Growth:

Stay Self-Aware: Regularly check in with yourself. What are you grateful for? How do you feel? Are your actions aligned with your highest self?

Nurture Your Inner World: Meditation, self-reflection, and mindful practices reinforce your transformation.

Live in Integrity: Your beliefs, words, and actions should reflect the truth you have reclaimed.

Protect Your Energy: Be intentional and mindful about what you allow into your space. Everything you consume (conversations, social media, music, environments) affects your vibration.

When transformation becomes a daily practice, you do not just experience freedom, you become freedom.

Consider which integration practices you are already doing. Do you practice daily self-check-ins? Regular meditation or quiet reflection time? Choose thoughts that align with your highest self? Set boundaries to protect your energy? Stay mindful of what you consume? Live in integrity with your values and beliefs? Celebrate your wins and acknowledge growth? Practice presence in everyday moments? Speak affirmations and "I Am" statements? Reflect on which integration practice feels most natural and which one needs more attention.

Design a simple daily ritual that helps you embody your transformation. How will you start your day in alignment? Perhaps meditation, affirmations, or journaling. How will you pause during the day to realign with your truth? A midday check-in, breath work, or moment of gratitude. How will you close your day with gratitude and self-awareness? Evening reflection, journaling, or meditation. Write your integration ritual as a commitment to yourself, something sustainable and nourishing.

As you do this work, reflect on what you are grateful for about the transformation you have experienced. How has your journey blessed you? Consider how you can love yourself more deeply as you commit to daily embodiment. What does self-love look like in your daily practice? And ask yourself what you need to forgive yourself for when you slip back into old patterns. How can you extend grace to yourself in this ongoing process?

Overcoming Resistance: Breaking Free from Old Patterns

Even after healing and receiving, there may be moments when old patterns attempt to resurface. Sit with this. It is an opportunity for deeper awareness and self-mastery.

Common Forms of Resistance & How to Overcome Them:

Self-Doubt Creeps In: Remind yourself of the beautiful work you are doing and that you cannot get it wrong and will never get it done. Enjoy the process. Use I Am statements such as, I am a beautiful work. I am worth it.

You Feel Unworthy of Your Blessings: Affirm, I am worthy and blessed to be a blessing. Release guilt and embrace abundance. I am filling my cup so that others can benefit from my overflow.

Fear of Losing What You have Gained: Affirm, I have a mind open to everything and attached to nothing. Therefore, I will enjoy the moment and embrace the experience.

External Voices Challenge Your Growth: Affirm, I am the creator of my reality and will stick to my script. This is my narrative and I own it.

The key is to observe resistance for awareness purposes without absorbing it. See it as an invitation to reinforce your "Knowing."

Identify your resistance patterns. What form of resistance shows up most often for you? When this resistance appears, what old pattern or belief is trying to resurface? Create a personal "I Am" affirmation to counter this resistance. How will you remind yourself of this affirmation when resistance arises?

Speak these "I Am" statements with conviction: I am a beautiful work in progress. I am worthy and blessed to be a blessing. I am open to everything and attached to nothing. I am the creator of my reality. I am always supported by the universe.

Then create three of your own "I Am" statements that speak to your unique journey and truth. Let them flow from your deepest knowing.

Living in Flow: Trusting the Unfolding of Your Life

Sustaining freedom and abundance means surrendering control and trusting life's unfolding. True alignment happens when you stop forcing and start allowing.

Signs You Are in Flow:

Life feels lighter; you are no longer carrying unnecessary burdens.

Opportunities and synchronicities show up effortlessly.

You experience deep inner peace, no matter what is happening around you.

You no longer chase. What is for you naturally finds you.

To stay in flow, practice detachment, holding desires without expectations. Allow yourself to be in awe of the ways blessings unfold. This does not mean giving up on what you want; it means trusting it will arrive in the best possible way.

Notice which signs you are experiencing in your life. Does life feel lighter and easier? Do you notice meaningful synchronicities regularly? Do you feel deep inner peace despite external circumstances? Do opportunities come to you without forcing? Do you trust the timing of your life? Are you less attached to specific outcomes? Do you feel supported by the universe? Are you in awe of how things unfold? Have you released the need to control everything?

Reflect on what helps you stay in flow and what pulls you out of it. This awareness allows you to course-correct more quickly.

Complete these flow practice statements: One thing I am ready to surrender control over is... One area where I will trust the unfolding instead of forcing is... One desire I hold without attachment to how or when it arrives is... One way I will practice being in awe of life's unfolding this week is...

Expansion: The Journey Never Ends

Personal evolution is infinite. There is no final destination, only deeper levels of growth, love, and abundance.

Every chapter of your life builds upon the last. Each experience shapes and prepares you for the expansion to come. As you continue evolving, ask yourself: What is this current chapter of your life here to teach you? How can you expand further into your truth and create value for others? What new possibilities are you ready to receive? How does knowing that you are always supported by the universe change how you move forward?

Embracing expansion means welcoming change. The more you allow yourself to evolve, the more you align with your highest potential. As you move forward, remember:

You are always evolving.

You are always expanding.

You are supported by the universe, always.

There are many creative ways to embody your truth. You might create a visual representation of all the "I Am" statements that define your highest self. Or draw or paint what living in flow looks and feels like to you using colors, shapes, and symbols. Some people design a week-long planner showing how they will embody their truth each day through specific practices. Others write a letter to themselves one year from now, describing how they are living in full embodiment and alignment. Choose what calls to your creative spirit.

So, I have a question... What does the most aligned, empowered version of you feel like, and what would it take to embody that version daily? Describe how the most aligned version of you feels. What shifts would allow you to embody this daily? What one action can you commit to taking today to embody this version?

Reflect on what you are grateful for about your ability to evolve and expand continuously. How has your growth blessed others? Consider how you will love yourself through the ongoing journey of expansion. What does unconditional self-love look like as you continue to evolve? And ask yourself what you need to forgive yourself for as you navigate resistance and old patterns. How can you offer yourself grace in this infinite journey?

Commit to one practice this week that will sustain your transformation. Perhaps morning "I Am" affirmations to start each day, your daily integration ritual, observing resistance without absorbing it, practicing surrender and trust in one area of life, or checking in with your flow state daily. Choose what feels aligned and notice how it anchors your embodiment.

As you close this chapter, reflect on the most powerful insight you gained about embodiment and integration. How does understanding expansion as an infinite journey change your perspective? What is one "I Am" statement you will carry with you every day? What does living in flow look like for you?

You are not becoming someone new. You are remembering who you have always been and embodying it fully. This is the "I Am" in you, emerging, expanding, expressing.

Chapter 10

The Infinite Journey – Embracing Life's Expanding

Healing is not a destination, growth is not a finish line, and freedom is not a one-time achievement. Life itself is an ever-evolving journey of expansion, discovery, and transformation.

Now that you are feeling, healing, and receiving, you stand at the threshold of something even greater: the infinite unfolding of your becoming. This is an invitation to keep connecting, trusting, and expanding into the limitless potential that has always been within you.

Take a moment to consider: What does it feel like to know that your journey has no end, only infinite expansion?

Remembering Who You Are

As we embrace this new way of being, we start to remember this as the life we chose. Before stepping into this human experience, we knew the journey, the expansion, the transformation, were all a part of our path.

Now, we are not seeking, we are remembering. No longer chasing concepts of light, we are embodying it. The connection made. The divine lives within us. We are awake to our true essence, and living from a place beyond belief, the place of knowing.

We have written our narrative. We have created our reality. You have walked through the fire. You have risen. This is your story; own it.

Reflect on what you are grateful for about the journey that has led you to this moment of remembering. How has each step, even the painful ones, shaped who you are? Consider how remembering who you truly are changes the way you love yourself. What does it feel like to love yourself from a place of knowing, not earning? And ask yourself what you need to forgive yourself for forgetting along the way. How can you extend grace to yourself for the times you lost connection with your truth?

Try this remembering practice. Sit in stillness and ask yourself: What truth about yourself are you remembering that you had forgotten or buried? Before you came into this human experience, what did you know to be true? Complete this statement from your deepest knowing: Before I came into this human experience, I knew that I was... Consider what part of your journey now makes sense as something you chose for your expansion. Reflect on how you will live differently now that you are operating from knowing instead of seeking.

Own your story by completing these declarations: I have walked through... I have risen by... This is my story, and I own it because…

The Art of Being: Living with a Mind Opened to Everything and Attached to Nothing

The most beautiful part of this journey is realizing that you do not have to force, chase, or control life. When you live in alignment, you move through the world with openness, allowing life to reveal itself in divine timing.

Ways to Stay Open to Life's Miracles:

Release Expectations – Expectations lead to disappointment. Trust that what is for you will present itself in perfect timing.

Stay Present – Joy and peace are in the now, not in the future or past.

Remain Curious – Approach life with the wonder of a child. Have a mind open to everything and attached to nothing.

Embrace Change – Every shift, even the unexpected ones, holds the potential for expansion. When you surrender to life's unfolding, you become an open channel for abundance, unconditional love, and new possibilities. Surrender does not mean passivity; it means stepping into your power as a conscious creator.

Consider which of these practices you are embracing. Do you release expectations about how things "should" unfold? Practice presence and mindfulness daily? Approach life with curiosity and wonder? Trust divine timing instead of forcing outcomes? Remain open to receiving in unexpected ways? Allow life to surprise and delight you? Surrender control while staying empowered? See every experience as expansion?

Reflect on where you feel most open and where you still grip or control. This awareness is the first step to greater flow.

Complete these openness statements: One expectation I am releasing is... One way I will practice presence today is... Something I am approaching with childlike curiosity is... One change I am embracing as expansion is... How surrendering control empowers me is...

You Are the Creator

You are not merely an observer in your life; you are the creator. Every thought you think, every word you speak, every belief you hold, and every action you take shape your reality.

Instead of wondering what the future holds, ask yourself: What do I truly desire? Does my belief align with my desire? What energy and thoughts am I radiating into each desire? What emotion do I want to feel, and how can I embody it now? What vision do I have for myself? How will I feel once my energy aligns with that vision?

As you step into your role as the conscious creator of your life, remember: You are limitless. The only limitations that exist are the ones you have accepted. Therefore, do not fear operating from a limitless mindset, it is your true nature and knowing.

Answer these creator questions with clarity and intention: What do I truly desire? Does my belief align with this desire? If not, what belief needs to shift? What energy and thoughts am I sending toward my desires? Is this energy aligned with what I want to receive? What emotion do I want to embody? How can I embody this emotion now, before my desire manifests? What is my vision for myself? How will I feel when my energy aligns with this vision? What action can I take today that aligns with this vision?

Speak these creator declarations with absolute certainty: I am the conscious creator of my reality. Every thought I think shapes my world. I am limitless, and I choose to operate from that knowing. I align my energy with my desires and trust the unfolding. I do not fear my limitless nature; it is my truth.

There are many creative ways to honor your infinite expansion. You might create a visual map of your journey from where you started to where you are now, including future expansion points. Or design a vision board that represents you as the conscious creator of your limitless life. Some people write a letter from their current self to their past self at the beginning of this journey, sharing what they now know. Others create art around the infinity symbol, representing the never-ending nature of their expansion. Choose what resonates with your spirit.

So, I have a question... What is life inviting you to remember, trust, or explore as you continue unfolding into the truth of who you already are? What truth is emerging? What trust is deepening? What exploration is calling? How will you answer this invitation?

Reflect on what you are grateful for about this infinite journey. How has your expansion blessed you and others? Consider how you will continue to love yourself as you expand infinitely. What commitment of love can you make to yourself? And ask yourself what final release or forgiveness you need to offer yourself to step fully into your role as creator. What are you ready to let go of completely?

Commit to one practice as you continue your infinite journey. Perhaps daily creator check-ins, morning remembering practice connecting with your knowing, living with openness and releasing expectations, embodying the emotion you want to feel now, or journaling about your expansion and evolution. Choose what feels aligned and watch how it amplifies your creative power.

As you close this chapter, reflect on the most profound truth you are remembering about yourself. How does seeing yourself as the conscious creator change everything? What does living with a mind open to everything and attached to nothing look like for you? What are you most excited about as you continue your infinite journey?

You have walked through the fire.

You have risen.

You are feeling, healing, and receiving.

You are remembering who you have always been.

This is not the end of your journey. It is the eternal unfolding of your becoming.

What is one final commitment you make to yourself as you close this book and step into your infinite expansion? Write it. Speak it. Live it. You are ready.

The journey continues. The expansion never ends. And you, beautiful soul, are exactly where you need to be.

Welcome home to yourself.

Conclusion

From Awareness to Action

The Triple Bliss: Gratitude, Love, and Forgiveness

Gratitude, love, and forgiveness are not just concepts. They are the foundation of Feeling, Healing, and Receiving. When the lines blur, and you feel lost, when life seems heavy and uncertain, let gratitude guide you home. Find something, anything, to be grateful for. Maybe your breath, the air that connects us all. Maybe it is the sheer fact that you are alive. Perhaps the trees, the rain, the warmth from the sun, the sound of laughter, or the small moments you once overlooked.

Gratitude is the way. It is the compass that realigns you with the deepest parts of yourself. It leads you back to the presence, to peace, to joy.

I remember the exact moment I felt this truth, not as an idea, but as a knowing. I was driving on the highway in Atlanta, GA, reflecting on my growth, and my commitment to healing and evolving. A deep sense of gratitude washed over me. As I looked over at the trees and the grass lining the highway, something within me shifted.

A connection I had never felt before arose. That connection was so profound and overwhelming that tears streamed down my face. I smiled, embracing the moment, the unity, the oneness.

No matter how many times I looked away, the feeling deepened. I was not just looking at the trees. I was the trees. I was the grass. I was everything, and everything was me.

That was the moment I truly understood being present. It felt so powerful and undeniable because I was present. Not dwelling on the past or projecting into the future. I was merely being. Then it clicked. Love, Angela. Love is the Answer.

What I was experiencing was not just an external connection; it was a reflection of who I am, who we all are. Love.

As I reflected on my journey to that moment, I realized that before I could fully receive love, I had to first unlock something within myself: Forgiveness.

Describe a moment when gratitude opened you to a deeper truth. How did it shift your perspective? What did this moment teach you about presence and connection? Let yourself remember and honor these moments. They are the breadcrumbs leading you home.

The Power of Forgiveness: Unlocking the Truth

To live in true freedom, I had to forgive, not just others but myself as well. I had to release the lies, wounds, guilt, shame, embarrassment, and narratives that were not serving me. Some wounds were buried so deeply, that they shaped the lens through which I viewed my reality. My reality was built on the shadows of pain, unworthiness, fear, and unhealed experiences. Healing meant turning on the light and illuminating those shadows with forgiveness.

From my free choices, I decided to plant new seeds of truths that reflected the essence of who I Am:

✦ Amazing

✦ Beautiful

✦ Courageous

✦ Divine

✦ Effective

✦ Free

✦ Grateful

✦ Happy

✦ Incredible

✦ Joyful

✦ Kind

✦ Love

✦ Magnificent

✦ Noble

✦ Open

✦ Perfect

✦ Quintessential

✦ Radiant

✦ Safe

✦ Terrific

✦ Unstoppable

✦ Victorious

✦ Wonderful

✦ Xenial

✦ Youthful

✦ Zealous

I spoke these truths, and I became them. In doing so, I unlocked the greatest realization: I was never broken. I was always whole, and so are you. Every experience carries lessons, and each lesson will birth a blessing. Knowing this invites us to ask more empowering questions, such as: "What is the lesson in this?" "Which gift am I here to share during this experience?" "What is emerging from within?"

Look at the A-Z list above. Which words resonate most deeply with you? Which truths are calling to be claimed? Speak them. Write them. Become them. These are not aspirations. These are remembrances of who you have always been.

Consider what you need to speak into existence about yourself. What truths are waiting to be claimed? How will speaking them change how you show up in the world?

Walking in Purpose: Sharing Your Light

Your transformation is not just for you; it is meant to inspire, uplift, and empower others as well. Every time you show up authentically, share your story, and express vulnerability, you permit others to do the same.

The world needs your light.

The world needs to hear your voice.

The world needs the fully expressed, authentic, radiant version of you.

So, a few additional questions...

How can you use your journey to serve and create value for others? What unique gifts have emerged from your healing? How will you share them?

What messages does your story carry? What truth have you learned that someone else desperately needs to hear?

How can you create impact, even in small ways, through kindness, love, and truth? Impact does not always look grand. Sometimes it is a kind word, a listening ear, a brave truth spoken.

Continuing Your Journey Beyond This Book

This does not mark an end; it marks a beginning. The truth is, you will never be "done" healing, growing, or expanding. You are an infinite being, and your journey will continue unfolding in ways more beautiful than you can imagine. You now know that you hold the power to create, expand, and move forward without limits.

Remember: You are a spiritual being having a human experience. You are here on purpose, not by mistake. Every step of your journey has led you to this moment. Trust it. Honor it. Walk boldly in your purpose.

So, what do you truly desire? What will you choose to create next?

Sit with these questions. Let them stir something within you. Your next chapter is already forming.

Truths to Carry Forward

As you step forward, carry these truths with you:

- You are a spiritual being having a human experience.

- You came into this experience Knowing.

- You are whole, worthy, and enough just as you are right now.

- Everything is as it should be.

- Everything it is, in your mind, it'll surely be in your reality. Meaning: Everything you hold in your mind will inevitably shape your reality.

- You are never alone; the universe always supports you and is always conspiring on your behalf.

- You cannot get it wrong, and you will never get it done.

- Everything is always working out for you.

- You are the creator of your reality. Create wisely and Own It.

This is your life, Live it fully.

Your story, Love it unconditionally.

Your journey, Enjoy its moments.

Choose three of these truths that resonate most deeply right now. Let them become your anchors. Speak them daily. Live them fully. Why do these particular truths matter to you in this season of your life? How will they guide your next steps?

Final Reflection: The Triple Bliss

Looking back on this entire journey, what are you most grateful for? How has gratitude transformed you? Let yourself feel the fullness of this appreciation.

How will you continue to love yourself unconditionally as you move forward? What does that love look like in action? Not in theory, but in daily practice.

What final act of forgiveness do you offer yourself as you close this chapter and begin the next? What are you releasing completely and forever? Speak it. Feel it. Release it.

So, I have a question... How will you choose to show up for the life you truly desire?

This is not a rhetorical question. This is the question. How will you show up? What will you choose? What will you create? Who will you become?

The answer is already within you. Trust it. Live it. Be it.

CLOSING BLESSING

You have felt deeply.
You have healed bravely.
You are receiving abundantly.

You are awakened.
You are remembering.
You are whole.

Go forth and live fully.
Share your light generously.
Love unconditionally.
Create boldly.

The universe is conspiring on your behalf.
Everything is always working out for you.
You are exactly where you need to be.

Welcome home to yourself.

With infinite love and gratitude,

Angela

LETTERS FROM THE JOURNEY

A Note from Angela:

On August 11, 2024, I wrote a letter to my past self. I did not read it again until April 11, 2025, eight months later. On September 15, 2025, I realized these letters were the missing piece of this book. They represent the raw, unfiltered work of Feeling, Healing, and Receiving.

I am sharing them with you, not as perfect examples, but as honest ones. You will see my struggles, my breakthroughs, my accountability, and my love for myself at every stage. My hope is that they inspire you to write your own letters, to speak to yourself with this same compassion, courage, and truth.

These are my letters. May they help you find the courage to write yours.

LETTER TO MY PAST SELF

Written: August 11, 2024

First read: April 11, 2025

Reflection: September 15, 2025 - This may have been the holdup! These letters need to be added.

Dear Angela Denise Hazelton, AKA Pooh, (past self)

I hope this letter finds you healed or at least on that journey. I just want to start by saying that I love and appreciate you. I need you to know that I appreciate all that you have done to keep me safe. You have been such a brave young lady, and I am in awe of all that you have courageously endured. Your efforts to keep me safe are admirable, but too much for you to continue to carry. I am setting you free today. Free to heal from all the trauma that life pushed upon you. You are so brave and strong. Because of you, I can stand boldly and face adversity. You have set me up pretty nicely. Your decision to accept this earthly assignment, knowing, is admirable as well. You have set the stage for a beautiful movie, and we, your present and future selves, will not let it be in vain.

I want to address some things that happened to you. The neglect of your parents were inexcusable yet forgivable. There was nothing wrong with you. You did not deserve to be neglected, overlooked, or mistreated. I know those are some feelings you attached to your rearing, and they have been challenging to replace. I know you felt unseen, and that left you questioning your existence in this world. You also felt rejected by your siblings at times, especially when you would walk into a room of laughter and your presence would yield silence from them. I remember you spent years thinking that something was wrong with you because they did not share the laughs with you. Baby girl, there was nothing wrong with you. That rejection, as you realized later in life, was God's way of protecting you from some of the drugs and alcohol that they were partaking in. That was not a part of your story. Which is why the present you does not drink or smoke. The plan was bigger than what you were able to perceive at the time. I am sorry that you took those things personal, and took it as something negative.

I want to thank you for releasing the incident that happened at the park. You protected me and I am grateful. I apologize for spending decades trying to make you recall something that you released in and with love. Thank you for showing me how to do that. I have gotten better at that because of the seed you planted so long ago. You are so brave and courageous. It is hard to conceive the reasons why I am not feeling so brave and courageous these days. However, as I write this letter to you, I am excited about the fact that I am you, you are me, we are one, we are we. I am brave and courageous.

Great job on that commercial you did, about the metric system, when you were in Kindergarten. Sorry I did not hold onto that information that you put in that work to recite. They sprung that last-minute opportunity on you and you accepted it on the spot and knocked it out of the park. That took courage and confidence, both of which you possess.

This is an extremely challenging paragraph to write. I feel a bit nervous and anxious as I type. Pooh, it was not your fault! The molestation was not your fault. He did not have the right to violate you, to threaten you, to manipulate you, to blame you for him physically abusing your sister. It was not your fault. There was nothing more you could have done. You were a child and should not have been forced to take responsibility or blame for being violated. I am proud of you for living through the trauma even though you were unable to release it at the time. You did not fully understand safety nor the fact that you were lacking it. The lack of safety left you vulnerable and someone took advantage of your vulnerability. You would be so proud of You today. You have created a platform that is a safe space for vulnerability, honesty and transparency. You decided to offer that space to help others heal. Wow! It is amazing to see this come into fruition. As I type this letter to you, I am even more proud of that part of our present life. It makes more sense why you/I/we signed up for these assignments. Let's Talk About It, Real Talk is the safe space/platform that has been created to help others. Also, Cardio, Core and Conversation is another platform that combines Life Coaching and Fitness. Let's not forget your book, Feel, Heal, Receive. Your decisions will serve amazing purposes and create value for others. I hope to make you proud.

I want to tell you that You are beautiful, always have been. I know you have always struggled with knowing your worth and value. Truth is, until very recently, the present you, was still struggling with it. We release self-doubt, low self-worth and inadequacies, in and with love.

I applaud your courage and willingness to give birth and raise six children, starting at the age of 16. Although it was challenging, you never gave up! As you grew older, you understood that assignment better, by and by. Kudos to you Angela.

BTW, you did not fail at any relationship. Each one was here to teach lessons. Learning those lessons, give you blessings that no one can take from you. You are an amazing mother, person, lover and friend and one day you will be an amazing wife.

This letter is my attempt to free you of any residual bondage that developed from birth to the present day. Everything is, as it should be... no worries, bondage, hate, anger, UN-forgiveness, strife, revenge, fear...You are free to be.

If there is anything that you want to ensure is completed, please let me know. I will do my best to execute.

I love You Pooh! Be free and fly high Queen Eagle, King Eagle is awaiting your ascension.

LETTER TO MY PRESENT SELF

Written: August 20, 2024

First read: April 11, 2025

Breakthrough moment: September 15, 2025 - Releasing 16-year-old Angela

Dear (present) Angela,

I know this letter finds you well and challenged. I love you. As I type this letter to you, I am doing my best to stay present in the here and now. I want you to know that I am proud of you. You have made and continue to make great progress. Do not give up on yourself. I feel the need to remind you that Gratitude is the way, Love is the answer, and Forgiveness is key. Whenever you feel a bit discouraged and are thinking of what you don't have, focus on things you are grateful for. You have come so far and don't give yourself enough credit for the progress. Stop for a second to just be present in this moment...

I have to address some things with you. This is not an attack; I'm just holding you accountable. You have been allowing yourself to get caught up in someone else's book. This is causing you to regress a bit. It is okay. Extend some grace to yourself and be aware. You are your book and have your own story to tell. You are valuable and do not need to compete with or compare yourself to others. Each person's story is a puzzle piece to this beautiful picture of the human experience. It is okay that you have not written your book, posted on social media, started your podcast, promoted C3, had an event lately, or planned one. Just be aware that you have beautiful ideals but a weak follow-through. Celebrate that it is no longer non-existent...just weak. We need to explore ways to strengthen it. Just like working out consistently will strengthen your physical muscles, you will have to work out your follow-through. What you are doing right here, right now, is working on your follow-through, and I am proud to share this moment with you. One thing at a time until completion and presentation. You will thank yourself for it, and your future self will also.

I want to acknowledge that I see you making steps towards connecting more with your femininity. I know that the explanation given about leaving your body during a traumatic experience and not returning really hit home. It brought clarity to your plea to be more in tune with your femininity. You are doing well caring for the whole of Angela. I am proud of you. You are consistent with your workouts and have stepped it up. You are doing well finding your mojo with your hair and skin. You are lining up the things you need for your follow-through and consistency. You are listening to your body as it relates to eating and feeling really good about that. You are spending quality time with your family and offering yourself to support the willingness of others to heal. That is major. Most of all, you are turned inward and working on Angela, Consistently. I am so proud of you. Your future and past selves are proud of you and grateful for the work you are putting in. It does not go unnoticed. Keep it up, and enjoy the process! Stay connected with your inner being/higher self/intuition! Do not become and remain attached to the outcome. Remember, that is the ultimate disruption that follows good intentions. Stay focused on simply enjoying the process.

Angela!!! You finally have your own place that is independent of your children/grandchildren. You have a two bedroom, two bath apartment that is clean, quiet, peaceful, safe, and furnished at this point. It is okay for you to embrace it. Stop fearing the future and be present baby. Celebrate your accomplishments, you deserve it. Also, stop feeling guilty about just being. If you would just allow, you can move on to the next phase of this assignment and celebration. Relax, release all reservations and inhibitions, and embrace your blessings. Think about what that looks like to you and go for it. Do you realize that you have not allowed yourself to celebrate the physical manifestation of your blessings? You have not celebrated paying your car off either. You have been so in your head about paying your credit card and possibly not going on the trip to Mexico, that you stopped practicing gratitude concerning your concerns. Just think about that for a second. I am here to remind you that you and God are the majority. You lack nothing! Your belief is that Gratitude is the way, right? What do you actually believe about YOUR beliefs!? Check yourself and allow yourself to be present in the moment instead of focusing on the past or projecting into the future. Here and Now is all that you will ever have! Also, stop focusing on what you See and pay attention to what is being Shown!

Just a gentle reminder that you share paths with your children and they have their own journeys. Continue to be consistent with your personal growth and self-reflection. They will draw from it in their time. You are doing an amazing job of allowing them to grow and offering support when needed. Your willingness to mend the brokenness and bridge the gaps is amazing. In due time, it will be accepted and received. Continue to master the basics of internal work. Continue to show them what unconditional love looks like. Continue to support the willingness of your family. You are doing very well and we are proud of you. We support your efforts.

It is now time to address your current relationship state. I mean your mental state about relationships. You are single and have been for a while. I know you get lonely at times, and that is understandable. I also know that you have been confused about this state lately as well. Well baby, Amor Fati - Love your own Fate. Continue to accept your current relationship state because it is what it is. It does not mean that there is something wrong with you or that you are not good enough! Continue to put in that Angela work, and it will all make sense in the here and now. Continue to become what you desire. Continue to date yourself. Continue to do the things you love and enjoy. Continue to release all limiting beliefs, including and especially the ones you have about being wife material! Know thyself and remain true to You. Be confident from the inside out. You do not have to minimize yourself or dim your light anymore. Truth is, you never had to do that. If your bright light makes others uncomfortable, that is not your problem to fix. Continue to be an example of self-reflection, intentional work, and self-development. This work that you are doing is prepping for the future You and she is ecstatic and appreciative.

Face your fears! Here and Now! I need you to take some time to think about and write out the fears that have been crippling you lately. The things and people that you long for clarity about, face it. Worst case scenario, they are removed. What is your belief about if someone walks away or if you lose something? Now answer this, what do you really believe about your beliefs??? Give yourself permission to be bold and courageous. Give yourself permission to have adult conversations that may be difficult. Give yourself permission to face those fears and move the fuck on...whatever that looks like. Take a minute or two to reflect on things/people you feared losing...How are you without them? Better right? It will always be that way if you truly believe what you say you believe.

I know you are contemplating going back to school to get your Masters and Doctorate. I support you as long as you have peace about that decision. Also, you have to have plans to progress your current ideals, even if you decide to go back to school. That is the deal! You cannot continue to let your worthy ideals lie dormant. It is imperative that you make moves and follow-through, consistently, one thing at a time until, completion. You have multi-million dollar ideas that are necessary for helping and creating value for others. This is not just about You!!! Trust and enjoy the process.

You are beautiful, inside and out! You have a wonderful spirit and a loving heart. Your willingness to work through challenging situations and offer yourself to assist others is admirable. You are a wonderful example of change, growth, progress, and resilience. Do not sleep on your capabilities! Let's Talk About It, Real Talk is your creation, nurture it! Cardio, Core & Conversation is your creation; nurture it! Now is the time to dig for a deeper understanding of why the Creator gave these ideas to you. Do your research and prepare to present and share your craft. You and the Creator are the majority. The Creator made you in its image and likeness...That means you too, are a creator. Trust your connection to the Creator and the journey you are on. As you continue to embrace your oneness, the naked truth will reveal itself to you. You are already equipped with everything you will need to fulfill and complete your assignments. You lack NOTHING!!! Allow greatness, because you ARE! Your voice matters, You matter! Soar Queen Eagle, the world awaits. I Love You Unconditionally!

LETTER TO MY FUTURE SELF

Still Becoming...

Dear Future Angela,

This letter is still unfolding, just as my future is still becoming. What I know for certain is that you, my future self, are already proud of the woman I am today. You are already grateful for the work I am doing now. You are already whole, free, and limitless.

I am not rushing to write to you. I am becoming you.

With every emotion I feel, every wound I heal, every blessing I receive, I am walking toward you. I am choosing you with each brave decision, each moment of self-love, each release of what no longer serves me.

I trust that when the time is right, the words will flow. Until then, I honor the journey between who I am now and who you are becoming.

I love you. I am doing the work for both of us.

Keep soaring, Queen Eagle.

YOUR TURN

Now it is time to write your own letters.

Letter to Your Past Self:

What do you need to say to the younger you who carried so much? What do you want them to know? How can you set them free?

What would you tell them about their worth, their courage, their beauty? What do you need to release them from? What do you need to thank them for?

Letter to Your Present Self:

What do you need to acknowledge right now? Where are you holding yourself accountable? What are you celebrating? What fears are you facing?

How are you showing up for yourself today? What beliefs are you challenging? What truth are you ready to speak?

Letter to Your Future Self:

Who are you becoming? What does that version of you know that you are still learning? What are they grateful for about the work you are doing? What do they want you to remember? What freedom has your future self claimed? How do they move through the world?

Write freely. Write honestly. Write with love.

Your letters do not need to be perfect. They need to be real.

It's A Beautiful Work. You Are Worth It

Today is the day, and now is the time
To honor yourself as one of a kind.
You have hidden behind the shadows of pain,
Pretending you carried no burden or shame.

But healing begins when you dare to feel,
To turn inward and embrace what is real.
You are not broken, lost, or wrong.
You have just forgotten where you belong.

You are not here by chance or fate.
You came with purpose, love, and grace.
A spiritual being in a world of form,
Born knowing how to weather the storm.

As without, so deep within,
Your truth lives under your weathered skin.
You are a beautiful work, not meant to hide.
Every scar, every choice, has been your guide.

Contrast sharpens what clarity shows.
Through every experience, your wisdom grows.

Gratitude is the way, your compass and light.
Love is the answer that softens the fight.

Forgiveness unlocks the door to peace,
Where heavy burdens find release.

You are free to choose, to feel, to be,
To process your emotions intentionally.

We walk our journeys, each uniquely divine,
Yet our paths intersect in perfect design.
We are all connected, woven by Source,
One with The Creator, navigating the course.

Decisions shape the life we live.
So choose the thoughts you want to give.
You lack nothing. You have always been whole,
Equipped for the climb, prepared for the role.

The mystery you seek is not external of thee.
It has always existed internally.

So honor the work, your path, your light,
Even when healing takes all of your might.
For what you carry, and what you release,
Creates the space for love and peace.

About The Author

Angela Hazelton is a heart-led visionary, emotional wellness advocate, and the creator of Feel, Heal, Receive, a transformative journey of self-discovery, healing, and soul connection. With a background in Health and Fitness Management and a deep passion for emotional resilience, Angela blends practical tools with soulful insight to guide others toward wholeness.

A firm believer that "everything is as it should be," Angela's work empowers others to embrace their truth, process emotions with compassion, and return to their limitless nature. Her unique voice is grounded in lived experience, spiritual wisdom, and an unwavering commitment to creating value beyond herself.

Through her "Let's Talk About It, Real Talk" events, "Cardio, Core & Conversation" sessions, and upcoming written works including It's "A Beautiful Work" and "The Seasons of ME," Angela invites individuals to feel deeply, heal fully, and receive life's gifts with open arms.

Her message is clear: There is Healing in Feeling and You are worth it.

Angela currently resides in alignment with purpose, joy, and divine flow. She is passionate about creating safe spaces for vulnerable, transparent, and honest transformation, one conversation, one breath, one heart at a time.

139

Connect with Angela:

hello@angiescamp.com | @angiescamp |
www.angiescamp.com

www.angelahazelton.com